MOVING AROUND THE WORLD
TRAVEL BY AIR

MICHAEL POLLARD

Editorial planning
Jollands Editions

SCHOOLHOUSE PRESS, *Inc.*

Copyright © 1986 by Schoolhouse Press, Inc.
191 Spring Street, Lexington,
Massachussetts 02173-8087
ISBN 0-8086-1026-0

Original copyright, © Macmillan Education Limited 1986
© BLA Publishing Limited 1986

Designed and produced by BLA Publishing Limited,
Swan Court, East Grinstead, Sussex, England.
Also in LONDON · HONG KONG · TAIPEI · SINGAPORE · NEW YORK
A Ling Kee Company

Illustrations by Hayward & Martin and BLA Publishing Limited
Colour origination by Falcon Reproductions/Scanning Gallery
Printed in Italy by G. Canale & C. S.p.A. — Torino

85/86/87/88   6 5 4 3 2 1

Acknowledgements
The Publishers wish to thank the following
organizations for their invaluable assistance in the
preparation of this book.

Australian Information Service, London
British Airports Authority
British Caledonian
Boeing Company
Cathay Pacific Airways
Civil Aviation Authority
KLM Royal Dutch Airlines
Lockheed — California Company
McDonnell Douglas
Royal Air Force Museum

Photographic credits
t = top b = bottom l = left r = right

cover: Civil Aviation Authority

4, 5*t* Flight International; 5*b* Australian Information
Service, London; 9 Flight International; 10 RAF
Museum; 13*t* James Gilbert; 13*b* McDonnell Douglas; 16
DPR Marketing and Sales; 17 RAF Museum; 18, 20
Boeing Company; 21 Civil Aviation Authority; 22 KLM
Royal Dutch Airlines; 23 British Airways; 26*t* British
Caledonian; 26*b* British Airways; 27 Cathay Pacific; 28
ZEFA; 29 British Caledonian; 30*t* KLM Royal Dutch
Airlines; 30*b* McDonnell Douglas; 31*t* British Airports
Authority; 31*b* ZEFA; 32 British Airports Authority; 33*t*
KLM Royal Dutch Airlines; 33*b* British Airports
Authority; 34*t* ZEFA; 34*b*, 35, 36 British Caledonian; 37*t*
DPR Marketing and Sales; 37*b* Flight International; 38
Boeing Company; 39 ZEFA; 40 Flight International; 41
British Airports Authority; 43 Civil Aviation Authority;
44*t*, 44*b*, 45 Lockheed — California Company

Note to the reader
In this book there are some words in the text which are printed in **bold** type. This shows that the
word is listed in the glossary on page 46. The glossary gives a brief explanation of words which may
be new to you.

Contents

Introduction

Air travel, which was once considered an impossible dream, is now a safe, easy, and fast way to travel. In fact, flying is much safer than going by car, or even crossing the road. People can travel by air from the United States to Europe in just a few hours. It used to take over a week by ship. Airplanes can also carry **freight** — from letters and small packages to horses and cars. Airplanes also help people save time and money.

▼ This Boeing 747 has an extra large top deck to carry more people. The cargo door is open. Freight is loaded into the plane on an elevator.

Airports

Almost every city in the world has its own airport. Airplanes land and take off both day and night. Some of the flights may be to nearby cities. These are called **short haul** flights. Small airplanes are used which can land and take off on short **runways**.

Other flights from the airport go to cities farther away or to other countries. Larger airplanes are used for these **long haul** flights. They carry hundreds of people and fly thousands of miles without stopping.

Famine Relief

When people are in trouble, airplanes can help them stay alive. In parts of Africa, rain may not fall for a number of years. Crops will not grow, and thousands of peole may starve. They will die unless food and help are brought to them quickly.

▲ Heathrow, London is a busy airport. This photo shows planes from eight countries.

► Out on a farm in Australia, a man has hurt his leg. The flying doctor will fly him to the hospital.

Airplanes from many countries bring in food. Doctors and nurses are also flown in to help. Sometimes, food is dropped from the air if there is no place for a plane to land. Planes can also take people from the dry places to areas where there are good supplies of food. Many lives can be saved in this way.

Flying Doctor

In parts of Australia, some farmers live and work in **remote** places. They are a long way from the nearest town and have to keep in touch by radio. If a doctor is needed, a radio call is made. The flying doctor comes in by a small plane and lands on a nearby field. When people have to go to the hospital, they are taken there by plane.

How Do Airplanes Fly?

People have always wanted to fly. Unlike birds, though, human beings do not have wings designed to lift heavy bodies. When you jump in the air, your strength gives you the **lift** to get you off the ground. The **weight** of your body, however, quickly brings you down again. Airplane wings are designed to give lift. In flight, they give enough lift to support the weight of the plane.

Modern planes are shaped like birds in flight. They have no flat surfaces to resist the air. This design, called **streamlining**, reduces the plane's resistance to movement, called **drag**. Even so, there is still plenty of drag. The powerful engines of an airplane give it enough forward **thrust** to overcome the drag.

There is a reason why a plane is shaped like a bird. It has to cut through the air as it flies. The air slows the plane down. It causes drag. The engine, however, pulls the plane forward. It gives enough thrust to overcome the drag. The weight of the plane pulls it towards the ground. In the air, the wings give the plane lift. This lift overcomes the weight. So the plane is able to keep on flying.

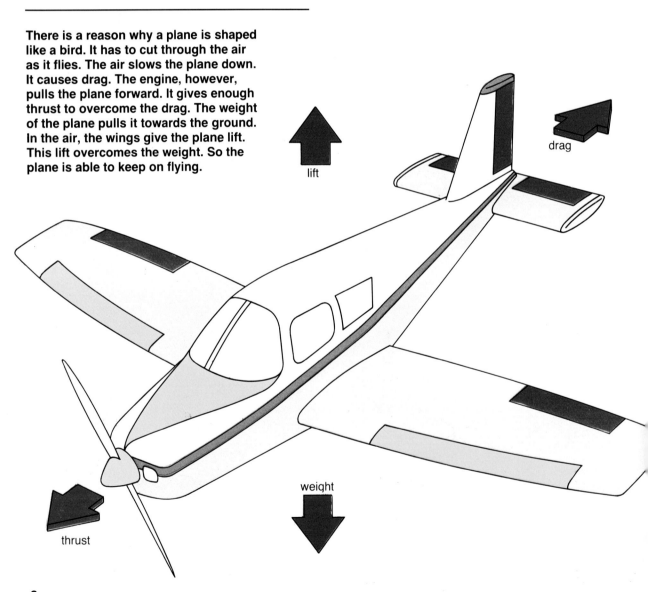

lift

drag

weight

thrust

The Airfoil

Airplane wings are shaped in a special way to give as much lift as possible. If you could cut a slice through a wing you would see this special shape. It is called an **airfoil**.

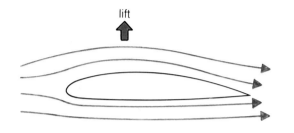

Wings are curved on top and almost flat underneath. When a plane is flying, the air passing over the top of the wing has further to go than the air underneath. In flight, the air under the wing pushes the wing upwards. This gives the plane lift.

Changing Direction

In the air, the pilot must be able to change the **altitude** and direction of the plane. The **ailerons** on the back edge of each wing help to turn the plane to the left or right. As one aileron goes up, the other goes down. The **rudder** is part of the tail unit. It moves to the left or the right. The pilot uses the rudder with the ailerons to make a turn or to **bank**. The pilot moves the rudder with foot controls.

The **elevators** are on the rear edge of the **tailplane**. They are moved up to make the plane climb and moved down to make it dive. The pilot pushes the **control column** forward to dive and pulls it back to climb.

▼ You can see the elevators in the picture. They are moved down to make the plane dive and up to make the plane climb. The rudder is used to make the plane turn left or right. The wings must be tilted at the same time. The ailerons on the wings make them tilt. This is called banking.

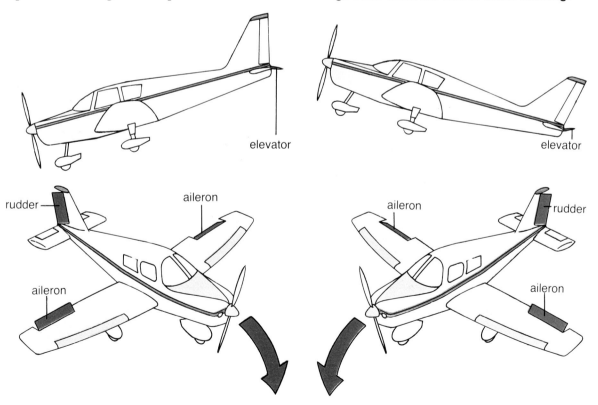

The First People to Fly

Nearly 200 years ago people made their first attempts to fly with **gliders**. These planes had no engines. Gliders had to take off from high ground before they could fly. Their large wings helped them to stay in the air.

The first gliders flew without a pilot. In 1849, the British **inventor** Sir George Cayley built a glider that carried a boy for a short distance. Four years later, he made one strong enough to fly a man over a small valley.

Otto Lilienthal

In 1891, a German, Otto Lilienthal, built and flew the first **hang glider**. He flew the glider by hanging beneath the large wings.

He could control the direction of the glider by swinging his body in the air. He made about 2,000 flights from a hill near Berlin. One day in 1896, his glider was blown by a sudden strong wind. It crashed to the ground. Sadly, Lilienthal was killed.

The Wright Brothers

In the United States, around 1900, Wilbur and Orville Wright started to make gliders. First, they worked out ways of controlling their gliders in the air. The wings could be moved to help steer the glider. The plane had a rudder which the pilot could move in flight.

No one had been able to fit an engine on a glider with any success. Some attempts had been made with steam engines, but they were too heavy. The Wright brothers made their own gasoline engine. It was lighter than a steam engine. They fitted their engine on a glider and called their plane *Flyer I*.

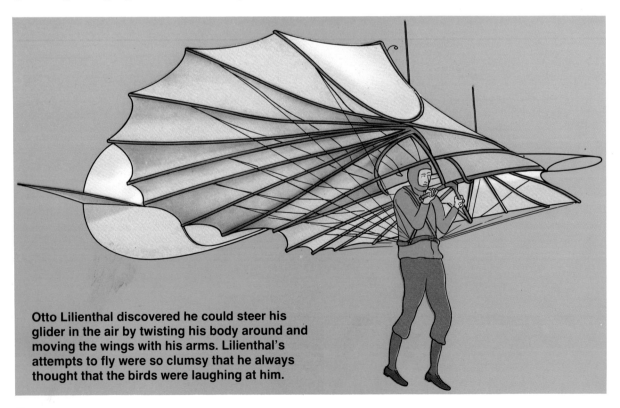

Otto Lilienthal discovered he could steer his glider in the air by twisting his body around and moving the wings with his arms. Lilienthal's attempts to fly were so clumsy that he always thought that the birds were laughing at him.

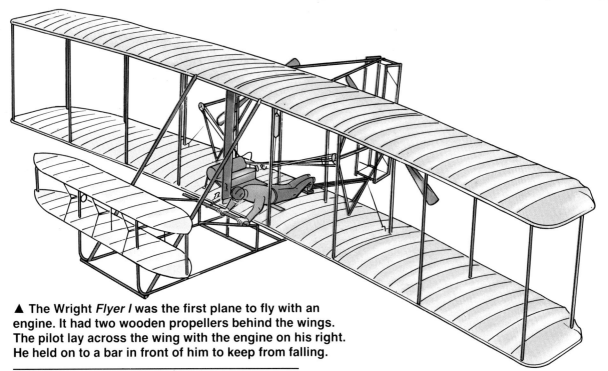

▲ The Wright *Flyer I* was the first plane to fly with an engine. It had two wooden propellers behind the wings. The pilot lay across the wing with the engine on his right. He held on to a bar in front of him to keep from falling.

On December 17, 1903, at the Kill Devil Hills near Kitty Hawk, North Carolina, Orville Wright made the first **powered** flight. It lasted just 12 seconds, and he flew 120 feet. Later the same day, his brother

Wilbur made a flight of 59 seconds and covered 852 feet. The next year, they built *Flyer II* and *Flyer III*. Each new plane was better than the one before.

By 1908, there were many other pilots and planes around. During these five years, however, the flights made by Orville and Wilbur Wright were still the longest.

▼ This photograph shows Orville Wright making the first powered flight in *Flyer I*.

World Flights

Lindbergh

At the end of World War I, there were plenty of spare military planes. There were also pilots who could fly them. Some pilots were eager to find out how far planes could fly. They also wanted to prove that flights could be made safely across oceans.

No one had flown across the Atlantic Ocean. In 1919, two British men, John Alcock and Arthur Whitten Brown, made the first **transatlantic** flight. Their plane was a Vickers Vimy **bomber**. It had two engines and extra gasoline tanks. They set off from Newfoundland and landed in Ireland 16 hours later.

The first person to fly the Atlantic **solo** — on his own — was an American, Charles Lindbergh. He took off from New York for Paris on May 20, 1927. His plane was called *The Spirit of St. Louis*. It had one engine and very large gasoline tanks.

Lindbergh sat in the cramped **cockpit** behind the huge main gasoline tank. This meant he could not see straight ahead. For much of the time, he was flying in the rain and in the dark. To make matters worse, he had no radio to help him. When he landed in Paris, he had flown over 3,600 miles. The flight took over 33 hours, so his main problem was staying awake.

▼ On May 31, 1927, Lindbergh flew on from Paris to Gosport in southern England. He was greeted there by Royal Air Force officers.

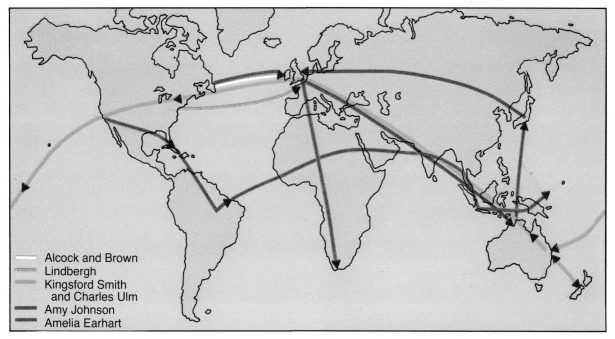

——	Alcock and Brown
····	Lindbergh
——	Kingsford Smith and Charles Ulm
——	Amy Johnson
——	Amelia Earhart

Around the World

Two Australians, Kingsford Smith and Charles Ulm, were the first people to fly across the Pacific Ocean in 1928. They had to make stops on the way. Their plane, a three-engined Fokker, was called *The Southern Cross*.

Among the first pilots was an English woman, Amy Johnson. She was the first woman to fly solo from England to Australia in 1930. When she made this flight, she had only completed 100 hours solo flying. It took her 19½ days to make the flight in her small plane, *Jason*.

Another great woman flier was an American, Amelia Earhart. In 1932, she became the first woman to make a solo flight across the Atlantic.

In 1937, Amelia planned to fly around the world from California. Near the end of her journey, her luck ran out. She was flying from New Guinea to a tiny island in the Pacific. Perhaps she lost her way or ran out of gas. No one really knows what went wrong. Her plane was not found, and she was never heard from again.

▲ The arrows show you some of the routes flown by the first pilots. Can you imagine how Amy Johnson and Amelia Earhart must have felt on their lonely flights across the oceans?

Key dates in air travel

1853	Sir George Cayley built the first glider to fly with a man on board.
1891	Otto Lilienthal made the first controlled gliding flights.
1900	The Wright brothers flew their No.1 glider.
1902	The Wrights flew No.3 glider, using a rudder to steer it.
1903	The world's first flight of an airplane with an engine and propeller, by Wilbur and Orville Wright.
1907	The first flight in Europe lasting over one minute, by Henri Farman.
1919	Alcock and Brown made the first flight across the Atlantic.
1927	Charles Lindbergh made the first solo flight across the Atlantic.
1928	Kingsford Smith and Charles Ulm made the first flight across the Pacific Ocean.
1930	Amy Johnson was the first woman to fly solo from England to Australia.
1932	Amelia Earhart was the first woman to fly the Atlantic solo.

The First Airlines

▲ The Handley Page Hannibal first flew in 1930. Eight of these planes were built as a fleet for Imperial Airways. They flew from Croydon Airport, London to Europe and Africa.

The first **airlines** to carry passengers and mail began soon after World War I. Many of them used wartime airplanes fitted with seats. In 1920, the first US air mail flight left San Francisco for New York. Many of the airlines we know today started around this time. They grew very rapidly in the years that followed.

The First Passenger Planes

The old bombers were replaced by passenger planes. These were specially built to carry people. The Handley Page Hannibal was a famous early airplane. It was a four-engined **biplane**, a plane with two sets of wings. Because of its shape it was sometimes known as the "flying banana." It could carry 38 passengers and fly at about 100 mph. Only eight of these planes were made. Altogether, they flew more than ten million miles without ever having a crash that killed anyone.

Soon, there were flights between many of Europe's large cities. Air **routes** linked the cities of the United States. People could fly all over the world. Planes had to land every few hundred miles to take on more gasoline. Because of this long flights had to be made in **stages**.

Flying Boats

After 1930, airlines began to use a new kind of plane. This was the flying boat, which took off and landed on water. This plane could carry more gasoline, so the plane did not have to land so often.

The Dornier DoX flying boat.

Most flying boats had four engines and carried about 30 people. The German Dornier Do X was a huge flying boat with twelve engines. It could carry 150 passengers and a crew of ten. On one flight, the Dornier carried nine **stowaways** as well.

▼ This photograph of a DC3 was taken November 3, 1936. The Gooney Bird had a thin outer skin of polished metal. Most other planes in those days were made of wood and fabric.

Still Flying Today

In 1936, American Airlines bought a new airplane. It was the Douglas DC3, sometimes known as the "Gooney Bird." It was streamlined like a bird. The DC3 flew at about 170 mph and carried 21 passengers. By 1939, nine out of every ten passenger planes in the world were DC3s. Five years later, over 10,000 DC3s had been built. Some are still used by airlines today. The Gooney Bird just keeps on flying.

Power for Airplanes

Airplane engines have to be powerful. They need to give enough thrust for take off and for flight through the air. Engines must not break down at any time. They have to be **reliable**.

There are two main types of airplane engines. The **propeller** engine is used to turn a propeller. The **jet** engine uses a jet of hot gas to thrust the plane forward. All airplane engines need **fuel** to keep going. Propeller engines use gasoline as a fuel. Most jet engines use **kerosene**.

Planes with Propellers

Propeller engines burn gasoline. They work the same way as car engines. In a car, power from the engine makes the wheels turn. In a plane, the engine turns the propeller.

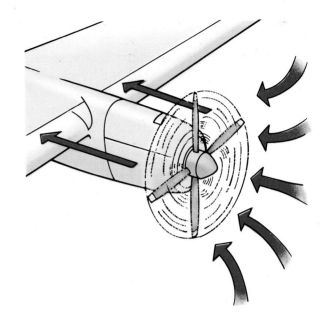

▲ A plane's propeller has two or more blades made of metal. At one time, the blades were made of wood. Each blade is twisted very slightly. As the blades spin, they force the air backwards. This fast stream of air thrusts the plane forward.

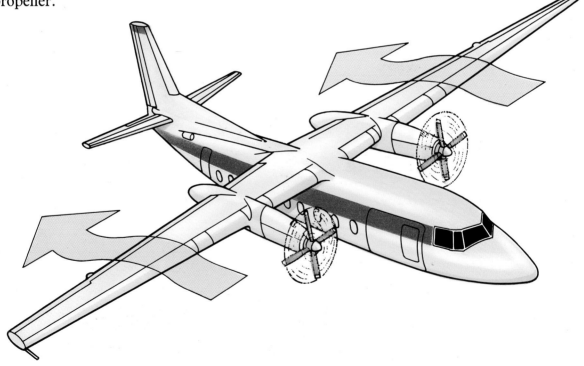

An airplane propeller has two or more blades. Each blade is slightly twisted. Because of this, the air is driven backwards as the propeller turns and pulls the plane through the air. The air is then swept over the upper surface of the wings. This gives the plane extra lift, as well as thrust.

A propeller engine is cooled by the air as the plane is flying. Propeller engines **revolve** more slowly than car engines. As a result, they are less likely to break down than car engines. They are more reliable.

Jet Power

Jet engines work in quite a different way. The jet of hot gas pushes the plane forward. Jet engines have fewer working parts than other engines and burn kerosene. This is cheaper than gasoline and does not burn so easily.

In a jet engine, air is sucked in at the front. As the air enters the engine it is packed very tightly or **compressed**. This makes the air very hot.

The hot air is then mixed with a spray of kerosene. The mixture burns as a very hot flame. The hot gases rush out of the exhaust in a stream. It is this stream of hot gases, travelling very fast, which drives the plane forward.

There are several types of jet engines. One is called the **turbofan**. The Boeing 747, the Lockheed TriStar, and the Douglas DC-10 airplanes all have turbofan engines.

The four turbofan engines of the Boeing 747 have to be very powerful. With a full load, this plane can weigh about 360 tons. The Boeing 747 flies its 500 passengers through the air at 600 mph.

▼ There is a large propeller-like fan at the front of a turbofan engine. The fan has lots of metal blades without much space between them. As this fan spins, it sucks in air. Another set of blades packs the air very tightly. The air is then mixed with fuel and burned. The very hot gases have to escape. They can only go backwards. They rush out of the engine as a powerful jet. This jet drives the plane forward.

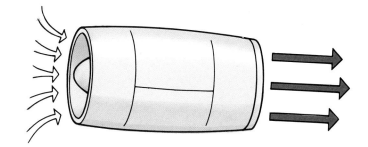

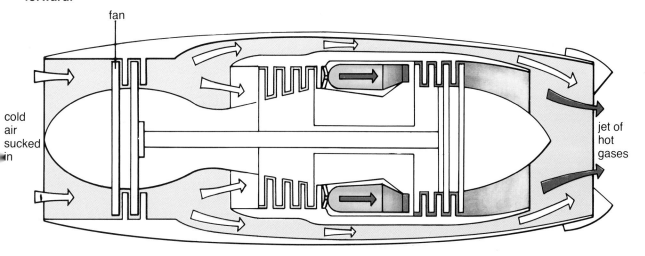

fan

cold air sucked in

jet of hot gases

Airplanes for All Purposes

Have you ever been to a small airport where there are very few large planes? Some of these small airfields have only short runways. Sometimes the planes have to take off and land on grass strips.

▼ This plane is a Dassault Falcon 10. It is made in France. It has two turbofan engines placed near the tail. The Falcon 10 can fly at 568 mph with these powerful engines. The plane can be used for many purposes.

On a small airfield, you often find a great variety of colorful **light aircraft**. They are used for many different purposes. Some people own their own planes or share one with friends. There are even air taxis. There are also airplanes available to rent. They are used by people who want to learn to fly.

Jobs a Plane Can Do

Small jets are often used to carry business people from one city to another. Others are used to carry mail and freight. Planes can also be **chartered** for a special journey or visit. These planes are hired, like a taxi or a motor boat. Charter flights often take people to meetings or sports events.

Special Jobs

Some work is easier to do from the air. It could take years to make a map of a forest or a swamp, working on the ground. It is quicker to take photographs from an airplane. These planes are specially designed for picture-taking.

Other special planes are built to help farmers. These are sometimes called "crop dusters." They use sprays to kill insect pests and improve the land. Crop dusters have to fly low and slowly because of the job they do.

In the United States, planes have been used to spot forest fires since 1919. Special planes have also been built to "bomb" forest fires with water. They are used to put out fires in Australia and North America.

One of these "firefighters" is the Canadair CL-215. It is fitted with floats and wheels. It can take off and land on the ground or on water. Planes like this are called **amphibians**. When a CL-215 goes to fight a fire, it scoops up water from a nearby lake or the sea. It can carry 1,200 gallons of water. It bombs the fire with water and goes back to scoop up more.

A selection of small passenger aircraft

Made by	Type	Country	Passengers	Speed (mph)	Range (miles)
De Havilland	Drover	Australia	8	158	900
G.A.F.	Nomad	Australia	15	193	840
De Havilland	Otter	Canada	11	160	875
Dassault	Falcon 10	France	7	568	2209
Israel Air Industries	Westwind	Israel	10	542	2870
Mitsubishi	MU-2	Japan	9	355	1606
Edgar Percival	EP9	UK	5	146	580
British Aerospace	BAe 125	UK	8	502	2683
Lockheed	Jetstar	USA	10	547	2994
Rockwell	Sabreliner	USA	10	563	1957
Gates Learjet	Learjet 35A	USA	8	534	2631
Beech	Super King Air	USA	13	333	1710
Antonov	AN-2	USSR	14	160	560
Dornier	Skyservant	W. Germany	13	202	652

Modern Airplanes

There are airplanes for every kind of traveler. Some large companies own their own jets. Their employees like to be able to fly in comfort to a meeting in a distant city. They can use a small jet like the Beech Super King Air. This weighs about 6 tons and carries 13 people. It can land on small airstrips.

Wide-bodied jets, like the Boeing 747 and the Lockheed TriStar, have made more affordable air travel possible for all of us. The 747 weighs about 360 tons with 500 passengers on board.

Jet airplanes have two, three, or four engines. The Airbus has two engines. It is a wide-bodied jet used mainly for short haul work. It can land and take off on short runways. The Lockheed TriStar has three engines. Two are carried in **pods** under the wing. The third engine is above the tail. The Boeing 747 has four engines.

The Distance Planes Travel

The distance that a plane can travel before landing to take on fuel is called its **range**. Some fuel must always be kept in **reserve**. This extra gas is reserved in case the plane has to change its route or is slowed by a strong wind. The TriStar is a long range airplane. It can fly over 6,000 miles without a stop. An airplane built in 1930 would have made about 20 stops to take on fuel to travel this distance.

▼ **The Boeing 747 has an extra upper deck to carry more passengers. It has four turbofan engines. Look at how these hang down from the wing in pods.**

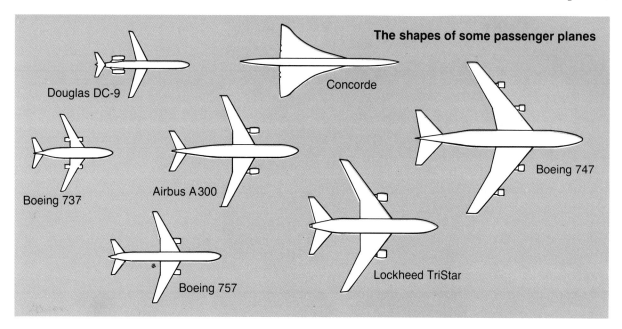

The shapes of some passenger planes

Douglas DC-9

Concorde

Boeing 737

Airbus A300

Boeing 747

Boeing 757

Lockheed TriStar

Flaps and Spoilers

To be able to take off, an airplane needs as much thrust and lift as possible. When it lands, it needs to increase drag to slow it down. These changes are made mainly by the use of **flaps**.

During take off, the flaps are **extended** from the edges of the wings. This alters the shape of the wings and gives the plane more lift. Once the plane is in the air, the flaps are taken in. When the plane is about to land, the pilot uses flaps. The flaps are lowered in easy stages and hang down from the wing.

Some planes also have **spoilers**. These are extra flaps on the top side of the wings. They lift up during landing and give still more drag. They act as brakes. A large jet touches down at about 160 mph. It has to slow down quickly to stop before reaching the end of the runway.

▶ On each wing of a plane there are two flaps and two spoilers. The flaps help to give the plane lift. The spoilers rise up and act as air brakes.

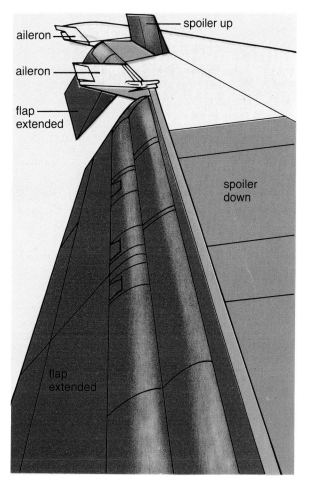

aileron

aileron

flap extended

spoiler up

spoiler down

flap extended

The Crew and Flight Deck

On any passenger flight, an airplane carries two kinds of crew. The officers on the **flight deck** are called the flight crew. They are the people who fly the plane. The cabin crew are the flight attendants who take care of the passengers.

The Flight Deck

The captain is in charge of the flight crew and of the whole plane. The captain always sits in the left-hand seat on the flight deck. The first officer sits in the

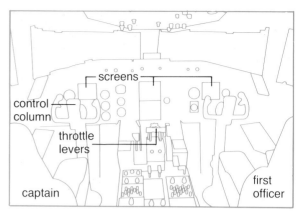

How would you like to fly a Boeing 757? The picture above will help you to pick out some of the controls and instruments. This plane has the latest equipment. Much of the information needed by the crew is shown on screens in front of them. These light up like TV or computer screens.

▲ The flight engineer sits behind the captain and the co-pilot. He has his own instruments.

right-hand seat. On large airplanes, there is also a flight **engineer** who sits behind the pilot.

The controls and **instruments** are laid out so that either the captain or the first officer can pilot the plane. They do not need to change seats. Dials in front of them show the plane's height, speed and direction. There are two sets of dials. One set can be checked against the other.

In front of each seat is a control column. Between the seats are the engine controls. **Throttle** levers control the power from each engine. Another set of dials shows how each engine is running. The two pilots can easily reach any of the controls they may need to use during the flight.

The flight engineer has another set of instruments. He or she must make sure that the engines are working properly. The captain must be told if too much fuel is being used during the flight.

Training and Fitness

Most of the flight crew's work is done for them by instruments and computers, but they must always be ready for an **emergency**. For example, they may have to land in fog, or an engine might fail.

This means that the flight crew must be wide awake and physically fit. There are strict rules which say how long members of the crew may fly before taking a rest. They all have regular physical check-ups.

The flight crew also has time off for emergency drill. This takes place in a machine called a **simulator**. The simulator has a flight deck which is a copy of a real one. Here the crew can practice dealing with emergencies without using a real plane.

Planning the Flight

Every flight is carefully planned. Long before the passengers **check in** at the airport, people are hard at work to make sure that each flight will go well.

The ground crew checks to make sure that all parts of the plane are working properly. Any faults reported by the last crew to fly the plane are corrected. The cabins are cleaned. Food and other supplies for the flight are put on board.

At the flight center, the **flight plan** is made out. This lists the number of passengers and the weight of the freight to be carried. The weight of the fuel is also given. The flight plan indicates when the flight will leave and how fast and high the plane will fly. The route is also worked out. The last item is the flight's ETA — the estimated time of arrival.

Briefing

The flight crew comes **on duty** about one hour before take off. The captain and crew go to the flight center. They look at the flight plan and are given the weather report. The captain will need to know what winds are **forecast**. If the plane has to fly against a strong wind called a **headwind**, the flight may take longer than planned. In this event, the plane will use more fuel. The captain will ask if fog is forecast at the other end of the flight. If it is too foggy to land, the captain will ask if there is another airport where the plane can land. Fuel supplies are checked. The captain may ask for additional fuel to be loaded.

The captain then **briefs** the flight crew. They will be told about the route and any possible problems.

▼ The captain and his crew report to the flight center. First, they are given the latest weather report. Then, they look at the flight plan.

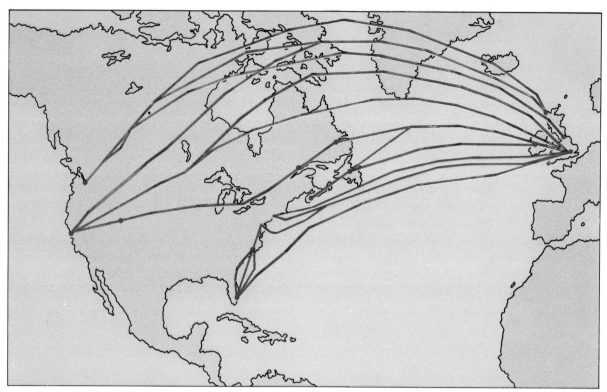

▲ Planes in flight have to keep their distance from one another. This map of the North Atlantic shows the corridors which planes have to fly along. The red lines show the corridors used by supersonic aircraft.

Pre-flight Checks

The flight crew then goes out to the plane. They begin the pre-flight checks. The passengers are not yet on board. The crew makes certain that all the controls and instruments are working properly. The captain and the first officer do the checks together. They make sure that nothing is missed. The flight engineer checks to make sure that the freight has been loaded properly and that the right amount of fuel is in the tanks.

The captain will also look at the passenger list and the cargo **manifest**. The manifest is a list of what kind of freight is on board. If there are problems, the flight will be delayed until the captain is certain that things have been corrected.

▲ Before the flight, engineers check one of the huge engines. The cover has been lifted to allow the engineer to look inside.

Airlines of the World

Airlines fly **regularly** scheduled flights. They fly on fixed routes. They have **timetables** that list the flights. There are about 500 airlines in the world.

The largest airline in the world is Aeroflot. It is owned by the U.S.S.R. Its planes fly all the routes inside Russia. They fly world routes as well. The smallest airline is Air Fret, a French airline. It has just one plane which flies one route.

Many airlines fly on the same **international** routes. They **compete** with each other, but they have to charge the same price for the same flight. They cannot cut the cost of the ticket to get people to fly on their planes. Instead, they offer better food, newer movies, or more comfortable seats.

The airlines have special ways of painting their planes. They have their own badges, or **insignia**. These insignia also appear on the crews' uniforms and in **advertisements**. You will often see airline advertisements in magazines and newspapers.

You will see 18 of the main airlines listed here. If you look through magazines, you may find many more. You could cut the advertisements out and collect them in a scrapbook.

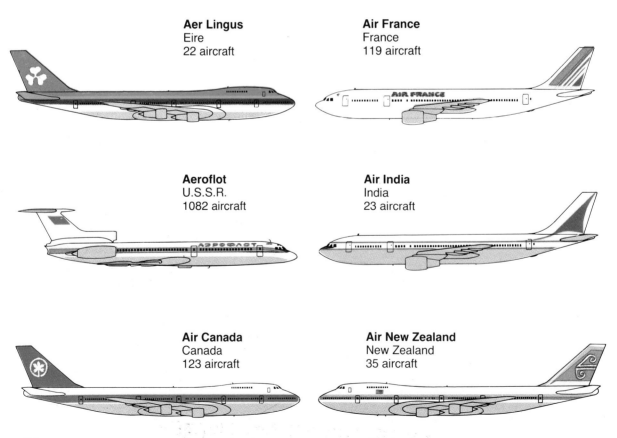

Aer Lingus
Eire
22 aircraft

Air France
France
119 aircraft

Aeroflot
U.S.S.R.
1082 aircraft

Air India
India
23 aircraft

Air Canada
Canada
123 aircraft

Air New Zealand
New Zealand
35 aircraft

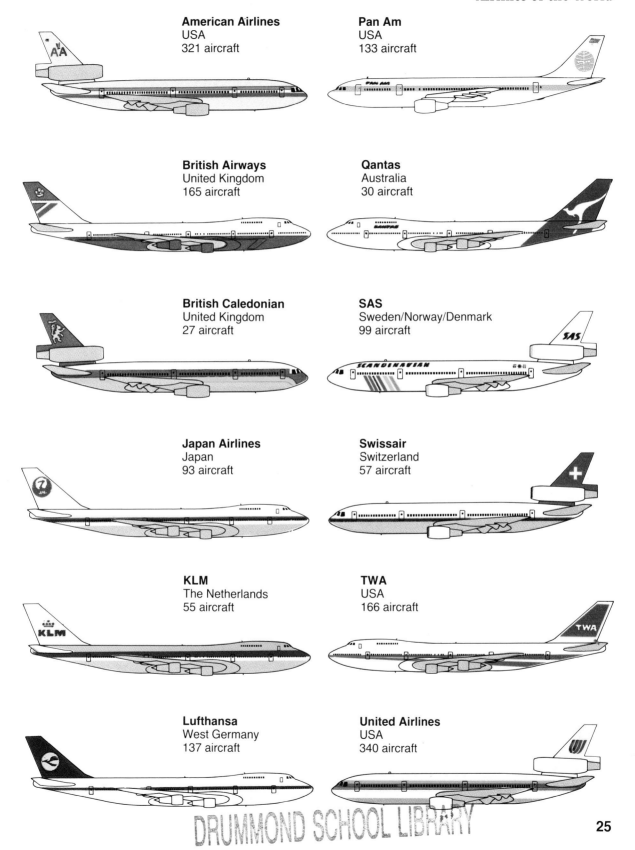

American Airlines
USA
321 aircraft

Pan Am
USA
133 aircraft

British Airways
United Kingdom
165 aircraft

Qantas
Australia
30 aircraft

British Caledonian
United Kingdom
27 aircraft

SAS
Sweden/Norway/Denmark
99 aircraft

Japan Airlines
Japan
93 aircraft

Swissair
Switzerland
57 aircraft

KLM
The Netherlands
55 aircraft

TWA
USA
166 aircraft

Lufthansa
West Germany
137 aircraft

United Airlines
USA
340 aircraft

Cabin Crew

Flight attendants, also known as stewardesses and stewards, make up the cabin crew. The first flight to have a stewardess was in 1930. She was a nurse named Ellen Church. She worked on the United Airlines flight that flew from San Francisco, California to Cheyenne, Wyoming.

Flight Duties

One member of the cabin crew stands by the door to welcome the passengers aboard. On most flights, people have reserved seat

▲ A flight attendant welcomes one of the passengers aboard as he steps into the plane. She is wearing a British Caledonian uniform. At some airports, passengers board the planes through a covered gangway. This is a kind of tube connected to the airport building. In this photo, the passenger has walked up stairs from the ground.

◄ There are baggage racks above the seats for traveling bags and other items. This British Airways flight attendant is helping a passenger to put away his coat and hand baggage. The plane is a Boeing 747.

numbers on their tickets. The cabin crew shows them where to sit. The crew makes sure that everyone is comfortable and that hand baggage has been stowed safely.

When all the passengers are in their seats, the cabin crew goes through the **safety rules**. They make sure that all the passengers put on their seat belts. The emergency doors are pointed out. Before take off, the cabin crew shows passengers how to put on a life jacket or **flotation device**. There is one for every passenger. Life jackets would only be needed if a plane were to crash in water. Above each seat is an **oxygen** mask. This gives extra air if, for some reason, it is needed on the flight.

In Flight

Safety is only one part of the cabin crew's job. The other is to take care of the passengers during the flight. Light meals or snacks are served on most flights. On long flights, the cabin crew will serve two or more full meals. A Boeing 747 may have up to 20 cabin crew on board. Caring for about 400 people is hard work.

▲ During the flight, the cabin crew is busy all the time. The Cathay Pacific flight attendant is beginning to serve a meal. On a long flight, meals help to pass the time. The boy is playing a game with his mother.

Some passengers may need special care. If they are old or sick, the cabin crew may have to keep a watchful eye on them. If the flight is bumpy, some people may feel airsick. Babies, too, will need special food. Young children may get bored on a long flight. If so, the cabin crew will try to keep them amused with toys and games.

Training

All cabin crew need to have some **first aid** training. Sometimes they have to deal with people from different countries. Being able to speak at least one foreign language is useful.

Flight attendants learn their jobs in full size model cabins on the ground. Then they help out on real flights with a senior member watching them. Even the senior crew members have more training from time to time to remind them of safety procedures.

Being a Passenger

Flying can be a lot of fun. A long flight, however, may seem very slow. The reason for this is quite simple. Most of the time you have to stay in your seat. Sitting still for several hours makes us all want to fidget. Even so, there are plenty of things to do.

▲ At Frankfurt Airport in West Germany, a Lufthansa flight is about to depart. Passengers are boarding a Boeing 737 through two doors.

Things to Do

Once the plane has taken off, you can adjust your seat to make it more comfortable. If you wish, you can stretch out your legs and go to sleep. Near your seat there is a control unit. It has buttons and switches on it. With these controls you can turn on a reading light or ring for a crew member. You can also plug in a **headset** and listen to music.

Movies are often shown on long flights. Headsets are used to listen to the movie **sound track**. This way you do not hear the noise made by the airplane engines.

When it is time for a meal, you can use a tray table which unfolds from the seat in front of you. You can use the table whenever you wish or fold it up to give you more room.

Looking Out

In a Boeing 747 there are more than 150 windows. If you have a window seat you can look out. At night, the lights of towns and cities show up clearly. They twinkle below you. On a clear day the land below is spread out like a map. As the plane begins to descend for landing, the map gets larger. Soon you start to see signs of life, such as houses and traffic. When you start seeing people, the plane is about to land.

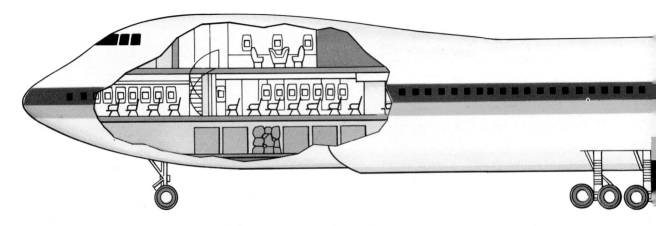

Moving Around

The Boeing 747 can carry up to about 500 people. The seats are arranged in rows of ten. In between the seats there are two **aisles** for walking around. You can take quite a long walk to stretch your legs. When the plane is full of people, however, it is not so easy to walk around.

The cabin of the 747 is very long. It is about 300 feet. The distance of Orville Wright's first flight in *Flyer I* was much shorter than this. He could have taken off and landed in half the length of a 747.

▲ This is just one of the compartments in a Boeing 747. In each row, there are ten seats. There are two aisles between the rows for people to walk in.

▼ The Wright *Flyer I* flew a distance of 120 feet. Compare this with the length of the Boeing 747. Things have really changed in less than 100 years!

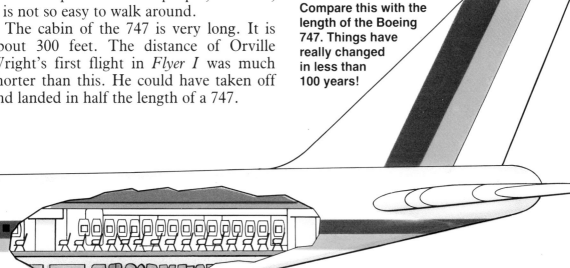

Air Cargo

Goods are carried by air as well as passengers. It costs more to send goods by air than by land or sea, but it is much quicker by air. Goods sent this way are called **air cargo** or **air freight**. Some airplanes are used only for cargo, but passenger planes also have cargo **holds**. Cargo holds are large spaces under the passenger cabin. Sometimes all the seats can be taken out of the cabin to make more room for cargo.

▼ This shows the upper deck of a DC-10. The passenger seats have been removed. Rollers and rails are attached to the floor. They make the handling of heavy freight easier.
In the small photo, you can see pallets on the left. At the other end, a container is being rolled into place.

Loading the Cargo

Airplanes cost a lot of money to buy and maintain. They can only earn money when they are flying. People and cargo must be loaded and unloaded as quickly as possible.

Goods to be sent by air go to the cargo **terminal**. Here there are large **hangars** where the cargo is sorted out for different flights. Goods going to the same place are packed into **containers** or on to **pallets**. Containers are large metal boxes made to fit neatly into the plane's hold. Pallets are flat trays with nets over their tops to keep the packages in place.

The cargo is taken out to the plane on carts pulled by tractors. Fork lift trucks and lifting platforms are used to lift cargo into the hold. Some planes have rails and rollers in the hold to slide containers into place.

Loading cargo into a plane must be done with great care. Computers are used to make sure that the weight is spread evenly. The cargo must not move about during the flight. Also, the plane must not be too tail heavy or nose heavy during the flight. It is too late to discover a balance problem when the plane is in the air.

All Kinds of Cargo

Many different things can be carried by air. Road vehicles or even light aircraft can be carried. A large number of zoo animals are flown around the world. They travel in holds fitted with cages. Racehorses, too, are often carried by air.

The strangest load of all was the space shuttle *Enterprise*. In 1977, a Boeing 747 was used to carry the shuttle "piggy-back." The shuttle was then launched in midair. Scientists found out how well it could glide back to earth and land.

◄ The nose of this Boeing 747 freighter is raised for loading. Containers are moved on the rollers to the rear of the cargo hold.

▼ The space shuttle was carried into the air by a Boeing 747 for its first flight. The space shuttle was launched from an altitude of 24,100 feet.

Safety on the Ground

An airport is an exciting place. It has to keep going night and day, every day of the year. Hundreds of flights arrive and depart in one day. Millions of people pass through one airport in one year. Safety on the ground is just as important as safety in the air.

Ground Crew

Hundreds of people work on the ground at an airport. Many are there to make sure flying remains safe. Before you board your flight, you will meet some of the ground crew.

There are strict rules about what you may take on a flight. **Security** crews see that the rules are kept. That is why your hand baggage may be checked by **scanners** before you board your plane. If a buzzer sounds it will be searched. You may have to pass through a special gateway. If you have anything metal in your pockets, an alarm will sound. You will have to show the attendant what you are carrying.

While you wait for your flight, engineers will be checking the plane. They will correct any problem that has been reported by the last flight crew. If there is anything wrong, the plane will not be allowed to fly.

The Runways

The ground crew has to check the runways continuously. They look for weak spots and loose objects. These could be dangerous for planes landing and taking off. At some airports, birds have to be scared away. They could fly into planes' engines and damage planes taking off and landing.

▼ A passenger passes through the security gate (on the left). If someone is carrying a metal object, a buzzer will go off. Baggage is scanned separately (on the right).

▲ A ground engineer checks the nosewheel of a Boeing 747. Landing wheels are always in pairs. This reduces the danger if one tire blows.

Snow and Ice

Snow and ice cause problems at airports. the lightest snowfall or hail can make a runway dangerous to use. Teams of people work all the time to keep runways clear of snow. They use special trucks to plow or blow the snow away.

Emergency Services

Airports have their own police, fire, and ambulance services. Teams of firefighters are on standby night and day. The fire engines can go very fast. They can reach a fire in seconds. The fire engines carry foam and powder to put out fires quickly.

▼ Runways must be kept clear at all times. Here you can see a ground crew at work with snowplows.

Prepare for Take Off

You can tell when your flight is about to begin. The cabin crew will close the airplane's doors. Then one of the crew will go to the front of the cabin and show how the seat belts, oxygen masks, and life jackets work. They will point out the emergency doors.

There is a warning light to tell you when to fasten your seat belt. It will come on before the plane has started to **taxi** out to the runway. You must keep your belt fastened all the time the light is on.

Up front on the flight deck, the crew will be checking the instruments. There are warning lights and buzzers to tell crew members if anything is wrong. The captain is in touch with the **control tower** by radio. The crew must not start the engines until the tower gives permission.

▲ The controllers can see in all directions from the control tower. They can talk to every plane on the radio.

▼ This DC-10 is ready for take off. It is being pushed out by a powerful tractor. Some tractors, like this one, have a driver's cab at both ends.

Now you can hear the whine of the engines. One by one they are started up. Tractors are sometimes used to tow planes out of the parking area. The plane may be towed backwards.

Taxiing

Special wide roads called **taxiways** are used to take planes to the runways. This can take quite a long time. The plane bumps up and down as it rumbles out. Planes are made to fly in the air, not roll along the ground.

From where you are sitting you may be able to see the wings. Do not worry if they shake up and down. They are made to bend a bit like the wings of a bird. It may be raining outside. A strong wind may be blowing, but an airplane can take off in almost any weather.

▲ At Atlanta Airport, Georgia, there is a constant stream of air traffic. The line of planes will have to taxi a long way to reach the start of the runway. Even then, there are more planes waiting. Each plane has to wait its turn. One by one, they are cleared by the tower for take off.

Lining Up

At the end of the runway, the plane may have to wait in line for its turn to take off. The captain waits for his orders from the tower. When your flight is cleared for take off, the captain lines the plane up with the center of the runway.

So far, the engines will have been fairly quiet. The crew will rev up the engines to full power. The noise may surprise you, but sit back in your seat and relax. You are ready for take off.

Taking Off

The engines are at full power, but, so far, the plane is not moving. The captain is holding it with the brakes. Then, as the brakes are released, the plane rolls forward. It gathers speed very quickly. The captain's eyes are on the center line of the runway. The first officer watches the instruments and calls out the speed to the captain.

If an engine should fail on take off, the captain knows what to do. Up to a certain speed called V1 (*vee one*), the plane can be stopped before the end of the runway. Beyond V1, the plane can still take off, even with one engine not working. Runways are long enough to give the captain time to make a safe choice.

Take Off

At take off speed the captain eases back the control column. This brings the **nose wheel** off the ground. A few seconds later the plane lifts off.

▼ The flight is cleared for take off. With the brakes on, the engines are opened up to full power. Then the brakes are released, and the take off begins.

You can feel and see the plane climbing. The cabin slopes up towards the front. As soon as the climb begins, the wheels are taken in. You will hear a rumble as this happens. This is followed by a thud as the landing gear doors close.

You will notice other things as well. If you can see the wings from where you are sitting, you can watch the movement of the flaps. You may find that your ears go "pop" as the plane climbs. This is caused by the change in air pressure. Chewing gum or swallowing will help your ears adjust.

Take off is very noisy. The engines are at full power. Some planes can be heard taking off from a great distance. Soon after take off, power has to be cut back. Too much noise would annoy people who live beneath the flight path.

In bad weather, the plane may have to climb through storms until it is above the clouds. As it climbs, the plane may bump and swing. This is due to **turbulence**. Once this turbulence has stopped, the seat belt warning light is switched off. This is to tell you that you can unfasten your seat belt. Now you are really on your way.

▲ This Boeing 747 is shown at the very moment of take off. First, the nose is raised and the nosewheel leaves the ground. Then, the other 16 wheels leave the ground and the plane is flying.

▼ Look through the window after take off. You can see the wing of the plane. You may see the airport below as the plane turns on its course.

Above the Clouds

During the early part of the flight, the plane continues to climb. Jets fly at altitudes of 20,000 to 40,000 feet above the earth. There are two reasons for this. One is that flying "above the weather" is smoother. The other is that flying at high altitudes saves fuel. Less thrust is needed to push the plane through thinner air.

The Air Inside

Above 12,000 feet, the air is too thin for easy breathing. It is freezing cold — colder than at the North Pole. The plane has to make its own **climate** so that people inside the cabin are comfortable.

The cabin is **pressurized**. Air is compressed and pumped into the cabin. This makes the air inside the plane like it is on the ground. Should the pressure system fail, you would have to put on your oxygen mask. This very rarely happens.

▼ This Boeing 747 is climbing above the clouds.

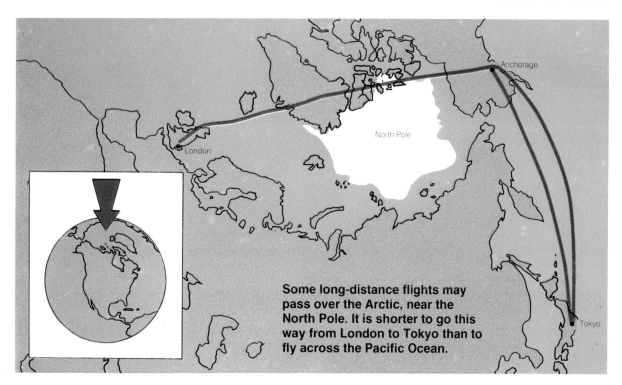

Some long-distance flights may pass over the Arctic, near the North Pole. It is shorter to go this way from London to Tokyo than to fly across the Pacific Ocean.

Finding the Way

Before take off, the crew knows exactly which route to follow between one airport and the next. There are no road signs in the sky! Instead, there are radio beams. Along the route from one airport to another there are radio stations on the ground. Each station sends out its own strong radio signal. On their **radar** screens the controllers see every plane as a "blip" of light. Radar beams are sent out in all directions. These beams bounce back off solid objects like planes. Even a flock of birds may show up on the screen.

When controllers see the "blip," they know which plane it is. They can tell which airline it belongs to and where it is going. Each plane has its own code. This shows up on the screen.

The plane also keeps in touch with each of the radio stations along the route. This way the crew knows exactly where the plane is. Computers are used to make it easy for planes to stay on the flight path.

▲ As the controller watches the screen in front of him, he can see the movement of every plane in his area.

Keeping the Air Safe

Air traffic controllers on the ground are the traffic police of the sky. They tell captains how high and how fast to fly. The controllers make sure that all planes are a safe distance from each other. Planes flying in opposite directions fly at different altitudes to avoid crashing into each other.

Landing

On a long flight, the crew starts to get ready for landing about 100 miles out from the airport. Now 'they are in touch with **approach control**. They are given a weather report. If there is fog at the airport, they may have to **divert** to another airport. If the clouds are very low, the captain may decide to make an **automatic** landing. In this case, computers are used to bring the plane down safely.

The Descent

At first, the descent is very gradual. You notice the engines are quieter. Some distance from the airport, the final descent begins. The seat belt lights go on. The plane loses altitude quite quickly. The

▼ This plane is just about to land on automatic pilot. The captain does not need to touch the controls.

captain is now in touch with airport control.

At busy airports a number of planes may be waiting to land. Only one can land at a time. The rest have to enter the **stack**. In a stack, the planes fly around an oval course, one above the other. As your plane circles, it banks often. You will notice changes in engine noise as this happens. Each plane joins the stack at the top. As your plane is cleared to land, the others all move down one place.

Landing

In the final approach, the captain lines the plane up with the runway. The landing wheels come down with a thud. The flaps come out further. The captain aims for the markers at the near end of the runway. Between the plane and the runway are other sets of markers. The captain knows how high the plane should be as it passes over each set.

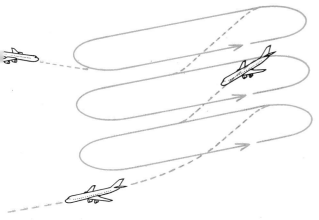

▲ When a plane joins the stack at the top, it flies around on an oval course. The planes move down one place each time the bottom plane goes in to land.

Just before touching down, the plane's nose is lifted slightly. The power is cut back. The flaps are now fully out. You can feel a bump and a rumble as the plane touches down. Then there is a roar as the engines go into **reverse thrust**. This helps to slow the plane down. You may feel the wheel brakes going on and off as the plane slows to a halt.

The plane then taxis slowly to the terminal. You have to keep your seat belt on until the plane has stopped and the engines die down. Soon everyone starts moving in the cabin. The passengers collect their things and fill the aisles. They line up to leave the plane. The doors are opened and the flight is over.

▲ The landing lights help the pilot to land, even in daytime. They can be seen through the thin clouds. The nearest lights in the picture are the approach lights. They are like automobile fog lights. The pilot points the plane towards the lights as he comes in to land. This helps the pilot to fly down the center line of the runway.

▼ Steering a large plane on the ground is tricky. Ground crew signal with paddles or lights to help the pilot steer.

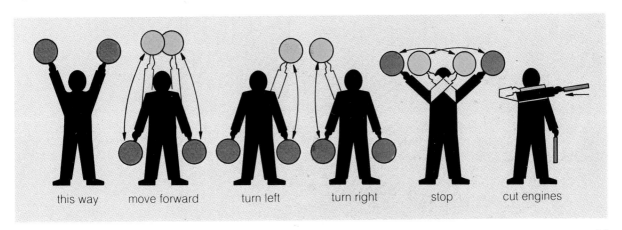

this way   move forward   turn left   turn right   stop   cut engines

Supersonic Flight

When a plane is flying it "squashes" the air around it. The air waves that it makes spread out in all directions. They are like the waves from a stone thrown into a pool.

If the plane flies at the speed of sound, something strange happens. The air waves cannot spread out fast enough. They build up into a **barrier** or a wall of air. It is known as the sound barrier. Ordinary planes cannot stand the shock of flying through this barrier. They would break up or go into a spin.

The speed of sound is about 760 mph at sea level. At higher altitudes, the speed of sound becomes less. Planes built to fly faster than sound are called **supersonic**. The speed of sound at any altitude is known as **Mach** 1.

Planes that fly faster than the speed of sound have a special shape. The nose must be pointed and the wings tapered. That is why Concorde is shaped like a paper plane.

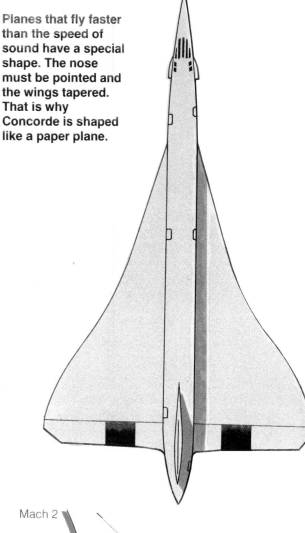

▼ When a plane flies faster than the speed of sound, it squashes the air in front of it. This makes a shock wave. At the same time, a loud noise like thunder is heard on the ground below.

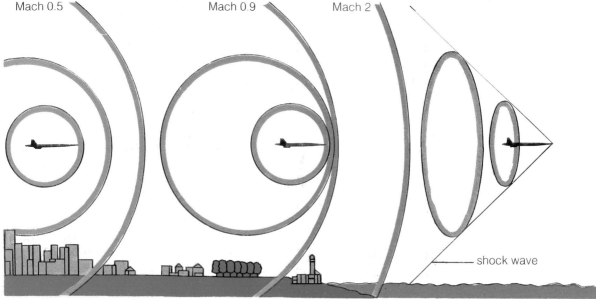

Mach 0.5   Mach 0.9   Mach 2

shock wave

▲ The nose of Concorde is slightly lowered for take off. It comes back up gently as the plane starts climbing. The nose is drooped down even more for landing. This helps the captain to see the runway.

Concorde

The first supersonic passenger plane was the Concorde. It went into service in 1976. The Concorde is designed to fly through Mach 1 without harm. Its wings are **tapered**. They are swept back to pass through the barrier easily. Also, the nose is pointed for the same reason. The nose can be moved up or down. When it is down, the captain has a better view of the runway. The Concorde flies about 9½ miles above the earth. Its speed is more than 1,300 mph.

At one time, people thought that supersonic flight would be the air travel of the future. No one thinks so now. When a plane breaks through Mach 1, the shock waves make a loud boom that can be heard below on earth. The noise can be loud enough to break glass. It can damage buildings and frighten people. So, planes can only fly at supersonic speeds over the sea.

That is not the only problem. Very powerful engines are needed to reach these high speeds. They burn a huge amount of fuel. The Concorde can carry only 128 people. This makes it very costly.

The Future

The Concorde was built by the British and French. Russia also built a supersonic airplane, the TU-144. It is not likely that any more will be built.

An ordinary airplane can cross the Atlantic in five or six hours. The Concorde takes three or four hours. Those who fly on the Concorde have to pay much more money for their flight. Most people choose to pay less money and take an hour or two longer.

Looking Ahead

What kinds of planes will we travel in 20 years from now? Some will be much the same as those of today. The Boeing 747 may still be in use. There will be some new planes, however. What will they be like?

For one thing, they will probably be no bigger. Anything much heavier would damage the runways. Airplanes will certainly be quieter, for the sake of those who live near airports.

New Fuels

Airplanes of the future will have to use less fuel. In the years ahead they may burn a different kind of fuel. The world's supply of oil is running short. The search is on to find other types of fuel for planes to use.

The Lockheed company has **adapted** a TriStar to use **hydrogen** gas. The hydrogen is loaded and carried as a liquid. In flight, it is changed into a gas.

After the year 2000, people may want the excitement and speed of supersonic flight. If they do, then these designs by artists might be the shape of things to come. The plane above would use hydrogen as a fuel. The design below is for a totally different kind of plane. It could fly above the earth, on the edge of space.

New Shapes

Airplanes are designed with large wings to give them the lift they need for take off. At cruising altitudes, less lift is needed. "Swing Wing" planes can partially fold their wings back. This makes them go faster and use less fuel. The wings swing forward again for landing.

Boeing designed a "Swing Wing" passenger plane to fly 4,000 miles at 1,800 mph. However, it was going to cost too much to build, and Boeing had to give up the idea. It would appear that the shape of airplane wings will remain the same for many years to come.

▼ This plane is also an artist's design for the future. It would be able to fly from Los Angeles to Tokyo in 2 hours, 18 minutes.

New Airports

Many short haul airplanes may use a new kind of airport called a STOLport. STOL stand for "Short Take Off and Landing." Planes using STOLports will have to be able to climb or descend very quickly. The runways will be short. STOLports could be built in the middle of cities instead of outside them. This would save passengers a lot of time. Today, it often takes people more time to get to the airport than they spend in the air.

The future of air travel depends upon what people need and want. The men and women who design and build airplanes will come up with new ideas. We can be sure of one thing. Their ideas and dreams of today will become tomorrow's reality.

Glossary

adapt: to alter or change something for a different use.

advertisement: a printed announcement offering merchandise, services, or property for rent or sale.

aileron: a hinged surface at the back of a plane's wing. It is moved up and down to help a plane turn.

air cargo: the goods carried on an airplane.

airfoil: the curved shape of a plane's wing. It is almost flat underneath and slightly rounded on top.

air freight: the goods carried on an airplane.

airline: a business which provides flights to carry passengers or freight from place to place. The flights are listed on a timetable.

aisle: a passage for walking between rows of seats.

altitude: the height of an aircraft above sea level.

amphibian: a plane designed for landing or taking off from either land or water.

approach control: the group of people in an airport's tower who are in charge of a plane when it is flying near an airport.

automatic: describes a machine or process that works on its own. Does not need human help.

bank: to tilt the wings and turn a plane in the air.

barrier: something which separates one thing from another.

biplane: a plane with two sets of wings, one wing above the other.

bomber: a plane specially made to carry bombs.

brief: to give facts and instructions.

charter: to rent a plane to a group of people for a special flight. Charter flights are often used for vacation trips.

check in: to report at an airport with ticket and baggage before a flight. You report to the check in desk.

climate: the usual weather conditions found in an area. Climate differs from one area to another.

cockpit: the place where a pilot sits to fly a plane. The word is mainly used for light planes.

compete: to try to do better than someone else.

compress: to pack very tightly. Air can be compressed.

container: a large metal box for carrying cargo.

control column: the lever used by a pilot to make a plane go up or down and left or right in the air.

control tower: the tall building at an airport where orders are given to all planes at the airport.

divert: to change course. Planes sometimes have to divert and land at another airport because of fog.

drag: the force that slows down a plane as it flies through the air.

elevators: the hinged surfaces on the tail of a plane. They move up or down to make the plane climb or descend.

emergency: an unexpected danger. It is an emergency if an engine fails.

engineer: a member of the flight crew or ground crew who takes care of the engine and other moving parts.

extended: pushed out. The flaps are extended before landing.

first aid: the help given quickly to someone who is injured or sick.

flaps: moving parts attached to the rear edge of plane wings. They help to slow a plane down for landing.

flight deck: the cabin where the flight crew controls an aircraft. It is in the nose of the plane.

flight plan: the written details which show where a plane is going, how long the flight will take, and other important facts.

flotation device: a cushion-shaped object containing air. When it is held or tied to the body, a person will float in the water.

forecast: a statement about what is expected to happen in the future.

freight: goods carried on planes, trains, ships, and trucks.

fuel: the gasoline or kerosene used to run engines.

glider: a plane without an engine.

hangar: a large building where planes can stay and be repaired. Cargo can be stored in a hangar.

hang glider: a glider where the pilot hangs underneath the wing.

headset: headphones which fit over the ears.

headwind: a wind blowing against a plane in flight.

hold: the place where cargo and baggage are stowed during a flight.

hydrogen: a gas which is very light and burns easily.

insignia: emblems or badges that identify things or persons. Airlines have insignia on their planes and uniforms.

instrument: a dial like a clock face which gives information, for example, about amount of fuel and speed.

international: from country to country.

inventor: a person who makes or introduces a new thing or way of doing something.

jet: a stream of water or gas that is forced out of a hole.

kerosene: an oil fuel used in jet engines.

lift: the force needed to get a plane into the air.

light aircraft: an aircraft which carries only a few people. Most light aircraft have only one engine.

long haul: a long-distance flight by an airplane.

Mach: a measure of high flying speed. The speed of sound is Mach 1. Twice the speed of sound is Mach 2, and so on.

manifest: the list of freight carried on a flight.

nose wheel: the wheel at the front of a plane.

on duty: at work.

oxygen: a gas in the air which we need for breathing.

pallet: a flat tray made of wood. Goods are stacked and carried on a pallet.

pod: a seed-shaped container. Airplane engines hang from the wings in pods.

powered: using an engine.

pressurize: to alter the air inside a plane's cabin. This makes it the same as the air on the ground.

propeller: a propeller is made of two or more twisted blades. As it turns, it pulls a plane forward.

radar: a way of finding out where an object is. Radio waves are sent out. When they meet an object, they bounce back to the radar set.

range: the distance a plane can fly without running out of fuel.

regularly: at fixed times, for example, every day or every week.

reliable: certain not to go wrong.

remote: far away from other people and places.

reserve: to keep back in case it is needed. Planes carry reserve fuel as a safety precaution.

reverse thrust: a way of slowing a jet engine down on landing. The hot gases from the engine are made to go forward instead of backward.

revolve: to turn around.

route: the way to travel from one place to another. Routes are shown on maps.

rudder: the hinged part of the tailplane used for steering.

runway: a long, straight track for planes to take off and land on. Runways are usually made of concrete.

safety rules: a standard method of doing things to protect people or equipment.

scanner: a machine which can check people and baggage for metal.

security: anything that gives safety.

short haul: a short-distance flight by an airplane.

simulator: a training machine on the ground which imitates flight in the air.

solo: alone, or by one person.

sound track: a strip along one side of a reel of film on which speech and music is recorded.

spoilers: extra flaps on the wings of a plane that act as brakes.

stack: planes flying around and around at different altitudes above and below each other. Planes stack when they are waiting to land.

stage: a part of a journey when a plane stops at an airport to refuel.

stowaway: a person who travels on a plane or ship without paying for a ticket.

streamlining: giving something smooth lines so that it moves through air easily.

supersonic: faster than the speed of sound.

tailplane: the flat, wing-like part on the tail of an aircraft.

tapered: pointed at the tip or narrow at the edge.

taxi: to move a plane along the ground.

taxiway: the roads used by planes when they move on the ground.

terminal: the airport building where planes arrive or depart.

throttle: the lever which regulates the speed of an engine.

thrust: the force of the engines which drives a plane forward.

timetable: a list of places that planes fly to. It shows the times of departure and arrival.

transatlantic: across the Atlantic Ocean.

turbofan: a type of jet engine which has a fan inside it.

turbulence: weather that makes flights bumpy.

weight: how heavy something is.

Index